CIVIL SERVICE

CIVIL SERVICE

poems

Claire Schwartz

Graywolf Press

This publication is made possible, in part, by the voters of Minnesota through a Minnesota State Arts Board Operating Support grant, thanks to a legislative appropriation from the arts and cultural heritage fund. Significant support has also been provided by the National Endowment for the Arts, the McKnight Foundation, the Lannan Foundation, the Amazon Literary Partnership, and other generous contributions from foundations, corporations, and individuals. To these organizations and individuals we offer our heartfelt thanks.

Published by Graywolf Press
212 Third Avenue North, Suite 485
Minneapolis, Minnesota 55401

www.graywolfpress.org

Published in the United States of America

ISBN 978-1-64445-094-9 (paperback)
ISBN 978-1-64445-182-3 (ebook)

2 4 6 8 9 7 5 3 1
First Graywolf Printing, 2022

Library of Congress Control Number: 2021945921

Cover design: Mary Austin Speaker

Cover art: Doris Salcedo. *Disremembered VIII*, 2016. Sewing needles and silk thread. 34⅝ x 16¹⁵⁄₁₆ x 4¾ in (88 x 43 x 12 cm). Copyright © the artist. Courtesy White Cube. Installation shot from *Doris Salcedo: The Materiality of Mourning*, on view at the Harvard Art Museums, November 4–April 9, 2017. © Doris Salcedo. Photo: President and Fellows of Harvard College.

for Chase, whose love frees form

Contents

what is possible, and where's the doorway of this room

—DIONNE BRAND

The writer steps aside for the work, and the work depends on the reader.

—EDMOND JABÈS

CIVIL SERVICE

The original gesture. The umbilical cord.

I: two bodies connected.

I eat for you. I breathe for you. I *I* for you.

My language can't other than host you.

Hosting is not always a posture of generosity.

Sometimes it is a posture of control.

I come to language having been expelled from your body.

I records my absence in you.

I records you.

Every time I write *I*, I am trying to get back to you.

Aren't you?

Is this a town square or a cell?

Difference is the meaning you make.

The poem is an event.

The poem takes place.

That makes the poem a geography.

The poem takes place in the meaning you make.

The meaning you make with what you've been given.

History is the compass.

Difference is the poem.

Let me say it differently:

Don't turn away. Here,

please, come in.

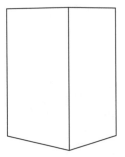

The spine of the book is *I*.

The book is trying to get back to you.

Can you hear what is flagging in the wind?

Wings, a weathered tongue.

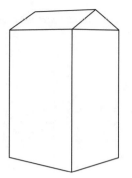

Is this a house or a cell?

Who locks you in?

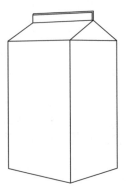

Inside the milk carton: *I.*

The town square, the threshold, the book.

The house, the host, the cell, the hormones, the history.

The geography, the poem, the meaning you make.

Milk is what happens inside the body.

Then outside.

Then inside.

It makes you well.

It makes you sick.

The cell reproduces. That is its nature.

There is no such thing as a free or reduced lunch.

The children are missing.

Can you see their faces here?

Do you consider yourself a part of or apart from?

Where you are apart from, what do you cast into the distance?

A poem is a line cast into the distance.

Now Amira is a part of you.

You are responsible for Amira.

Here we are.

She's in your hands now.

Of course, Amira is wanted.

[AMIRA LOOKS AT THE WALL.]

What is the meaning of life?

We enlarge it with our grief.

Death Revises Badly

In the Old Dictator's obituary, a charming anecdote—

When the Old Dictator was a boy, his father saved his wages
for a month to buy his son a watch. The boy, in turn,
turned back the watch's hands every day for a month
so his father would not lose time on his account.

Remember—

Before he was the Old Dictator, he was a baby
babbling. Now he speaks three languages,
thanks to his time in the army. After genocide,
he took up painting. "His paintings manifest a man
grappling," the Curator attests, buys seven.

When the Dictator scorned the Old Dictator,
the townspeople awarded the Old Dictator
a new title: Empathetic.

"Look at that soft power," a townswoman cooed.
"Bruised like peaches from the half-off bin."

The townspeople collected their best language
to offer the Empathetic Dictator.
The Empathetic Dictator was not home.
(He had gone to play golf with the Dictator.)

The townspeople left their gift on his stoop.

When the Empathetic Dictator returned, he adorned himself
with the townspeople's best language. He commissioned a photo,
which he had made into Christmas cards. The townspeople
displayed the cards on their mantelpieces.

One day, the photo finds the homepage. *The Empathetic Dictator has died,* the newspaper reports. *The townspeople are sad.* The townspeople read of their sadness on tiny screens.

How tender the old rule appears when you hold it up to the present like a cashier turning a hundred-dollar bill toward the light, squinting, proclaiming it *Real.*

Perennial

The Archivist walks out of the book
and into evening early. On his street, the houses
line up like good teeth. The Archivist's neighbor
misses his wife. Thirty years ago, she quit
the house and the twilight swallowed her.
Still searching, the neighbor
opens the belly of the neighborhood cat.
The Archivist, mind fast
to his research, passes the plundered animal by.
Books clutter his seeing. The knife, a better eye.
The flowers are screaming
the old scream. The Archivist opens his mouth
to join them. The scream clarifies an elsewhere.
He saw the flowers there.
The tulips were red.

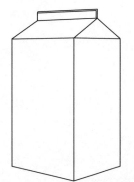

[Amira sits at the table, stares straight ahead.]

Does torture produce intelligence?

It produces the forms of fact.

Do you call that intelligence?

Lecture on Time

On the clock, the face reveals the hand.
The hand reveals—the woman is late.
She flees her apartment enlarged by scarves and perfume.

     It's true. The juice of a boiled carrot
          can drag a body through a week.

Time is contagious.
Fire in a dry forest.
G-dless branches, this time.

Amira stole pruning shears from a neighbor's shed.
Cut a hole in the dusk. Huddled in the hole, hungry.

If you could, for five minutes,
withhold the world—what then?

That spring, the roses went rogue.

Indecipherable hour: smallest of morning's rooms.

     Coffee unlocks the senses.
     A door in the day.

Only time was brittle, only the ice underfoot.
Something broke.
The woman's lover left a note.

Each person has a story.
     Each story is a tragedy.
     Tragedy is a question of time.

Red flares over the river.

Rot records a past.

There is no such thing as forever.
            The snow dreamt it up.

They say the past has become unpredictable.

The Institute of Horology loses accreditation.

Having lost their jobs, the horologists lose
their houses. They live under a bridge,
steadfast water rushing past their feet
on its way home.

                A thousand filthy cuckoos
                burst forth, swelling the meantime like a song.

A lifetime is what transpires until the document concludes it.

        A conversation interrupted by the bell's indifferent toll.

                            "Your fragile geometries of enclosure,
                    feeble instruments, pathological monuments.
                            Don't you know any other way?"

You cannot solve time, even with death.

The only clue is pleasure.

The answer presents a set of questions
like a clown whipping a bouquet of plastic flowers
from behind his back, scattering the children.

From bloom to snow, a woman sings the old song to her belly.
The baby greets the world headfirst,
breath pocked with shimmering glyphs.

Your breath takes residence in her.
That's how she knows it is time.

The grammar out doesn't occur to her here.

The prisoner
                    knows she will die inside this sentence.
The writer

"I write this in a stranger's hand."

Where the state does not recognize
your sentence, your sentence
is administered by the state. Which is to say:
the state administers your sentence
whether you recognize it or not.

Or not.

The poem won't release you.

On TV, impeccable teeth report
the results recorded the evening before voting.

The Creditor buys up the futures
the townspeople will spend
paying for their pasts.

Interminable roster of presents.

Tenseless grace of infinitives.

To destroy history and believe
there will be human witness left to assemble
this time in language.

> To believe that language would exonerate you.
> To corrode meaning with your delusion.

"I eradicate infinity with my life."

For its brief spell, the body catches time.
Then time discards the body, moves on.

> To be alive is to be suspended
>   in G-d's sentence
>   like a spider in amber.

Amira is knocking on the outside of your hour.

The flowers are not in season.

How ill-fated to arrive empty-handed
                        to your funeral.

Only the stars flinch.

The fires diminish.
The elements refuse.

An old woman puts her slippers on her hands,
her hands on the red cheeks of her grandson, singing—

> *Apple, apple from the tree. I'll pluck one*
>   *from the highest branch and stitch it into your face*
>   *for safekeeping.*

In her language, the song rhymes.

Her grandson wonders absently
after this foreign fruit.
      His wondering is an insect
        skittering across the floor of his mind.

Your hung head, a syllable of sorrow.

The night, dense with time.

      Death is time passed through a star.

        I is always trying to make a point
        of *you* so *I* can locate itself.

Your way is what precedes you.

We can other now, only no one wants to. No one:
the one who wants, who lives out from time.

Amira is no one.
The proof is in the petals.

A way out: to be with, otherwise.

Who hasn't felt freed in the presence
of someone's deep thinking?

      Art is not use, but the other thing.
        Not the spoon, but the carving on its handle.

        Beauty scoops you from time, useless.

Waiting for a lover's call, a woman feeds time to a meat grinder.

To grieve is to long
to obliterate the future
which is everywhere
the dead are no longer
responsive to their human names.

       Beneath a willow, a woman in lace
       weeps for her language's lessening.

                  Amira pulls the hours around her like a shawl.

The past is only the past because the present
needs somewhere to point its crooked finger.

The way *I* is *you*, is not, knots itself—*I I I I I*
       I, solitary, loosed from *you*, loses all sense
       of time, collates the ends into a circle. Loop
       of thought, evasion of syntax.

       The syntax makes the subject.
       You are subjected to inclusion.

                  Amira loiters outside.
                    Lavish vagrancy.

That the sentence eludes the prisoner is the sentence:
doing time—no matter. No matter the sentence
predicated this future into being. The torture is sentenced,
is time.

Palliative freedom forestalls freedom time.

       On top of every cell, the eye of G-d.

       Waiting rooms bloated with light.

In the cell, a fluorescent bulb
cleaves the sun from the prisoner
who has not, in thirty-five years, seen a star,
who apprehends the outside by rising up,
six-hundred-year-old light
barreling toward her. It's too much to bear—
how the past presents itself.

The star's speech: snapshot of a mouth long gone.

The townspeople rub the days together like sticks.

"The future light will still hold you."

In the Holy City, buildings made from stone
bearing the city's colonial name. Colonizers settling
into old gods. Old gods tilling the barren fields.

The factory made time.
We wage time.
Time wages us. Wage times us.

After all that time, the carrots were bad.

History opened like a hand—like repentant children,
we put everything good there.

Apples

The townspeople paste wax apples on the trees,
glow shyly out their windows as the Dictator
struts past the monument of his father strutting
past nothing at all. Yesterday, the Dictator dressed
the Butcher's boy in the uniform of his own son.
Today, at the orders of the Dictator, guards shot the boy.

In the town of his childhood, the Curator is a tourist.
He touches his mother with the language
with which he does not touch his work.
In the painting, bored bored Eve chomps on an apple.
In the tongue of his work, he acquires her.

At the banquet: music wrung from the townspeople's anguish,
pigs choked with apples.
The meat in the soup is human meat.
The Dictator's rings are made of gold
yanked from the teeth of corpses.

The Censor bloats with what he knows.
His sons bloom in neat rows.
An orchard grows inside his wife.
He prunes her on Sundays.

Under the earth, the Butcher's boy, laughing,
eats an apple. The core rises, light with rot.
The Dictator admires the fruit of his land.

Preferential Treatment

The Censor uses the black crayon
to eradicate sex. On payday, he takes
his wife and son to Shake Shack. *Whatever
you want*, the Censor says to his wife
when she asks what she should have.
The Censor crosses *provide for your family*
off the list he keeps tucked in his billfold. To track
the time, the Censor sings "You Are My Sunshine" twice
while his son brushes his teeth. The boy shows the glass
his shining mouthstones and growls. He is a bear. No,
he is a boy. In the boy's drawings, the zebras
are purple and white. His mother hangs
them on the fridge. *What beautiful horses*,
the Censor says. His wife's wit trembles, then ebbs.
The children's nails are clogged with black wax.

Meaning Well

We have come together, the Board Chair begins,
for obvious reasons. In a time of great division, this table—
he raps his knuckles against the oak
for emphasis—*is a metaphor*. In another room,
in another country, the Lumberjack laughs tightly
through his teeth, pain scaling his spine,
sharp as the word a man deploys
to cleave the thick silence that follows
a lovers' quarrel. Nothing proliferates metaphor
like love. Nothing severs word from symbol like pain.
Like pain is a truncated simile; without tenor.
During the war, the Board Chair sings
of business as usual. Without which,
the Chair has no job. (Without business as usual,
or without the war? Name the difference.) *Unfortunately,*
that's not realistic, the Chair replies to a proposal
from a woman whose name he refuses
to pronounce. The Real endowed the Chair
with two houses and a boat, which his daughters borrow
on Sundays each August. The Chair says *I hear you*
three times, and the woman's speech is barricaded
behind his declaration. Now when she opens her mouth,
money flies out. The money is embossed
with the Dictator's face. From a baroque frame
on the boardroom wall, the Dictator's father
looks on sternly. His head hangs above the Board Chair.
Perhaps he misses his table. *Perhaps this meeting*
has always been my life, the Curator thinks, staring blankly
at the toddler whose face wallpapers his phone.
Every hour in this room, a brick
in the rampart against bright thought.
n rspns t th rcnt vnts tht rmnd s tht rcsm xsts n ll spcts
f prsnl nd prfssnl lf, the Stenographer records dutifully,

w wll mv t stblsh th Frdm Grnt. The Dictator
put his face on the language like he put his face
on the money. The Stenographer is struggling
to keep up. She was up late, irritated by heartbreak.
The common animal of her innards disgusts her.
The cold region of her childhood lives
in her vowels. She keeps her mouth shut.
The Board Chair is satisfied with what they've accomplished.

Orderly Conduct

who wrung your hands
who rung up your lacy underwear
who tailored your tongue
who danced for the patron
who didn't masturbate for forty days
who detonated the bath bomb
whose free two-day shipping
whose pomp and imposter syndrome
whose hearts and mines
who applauded the veterans boarding the plane
who hate-read the article
whose title increased
whose art war makes
who took the meeting anyway
whose question was really more of a comment
whose difference of opinion
whose yard sign believed in love
whose kitchen was furnished with tiles from a bathhouse
who brunched about thread count
whose good deed goes

[Amira sits at the table. her back does not touch the chair.]

What do you do with what you know?

What do you see when you look at me?

What is the point of visibility?

It recedes into the distance.

Diet

Someone has eaten the Intern's yogurt again.
The Intern looks at the Stenographer's belly,

wondering. The Stenographer has given up gluten
and hopes for a baby. "Did you eat my yogurt?"

the Intern asks. Questions are not in the Stenographer's realm
of responsibility. The Intern regrets increasing her debt

by the bloated cost of a Sharpie, sold individually
next to the register at the pharmacy where

the Intern gets her Lexapro. "I wrote my name on it,"
the Intern says, mustering, she hopes, something

her mother calls *sense of self*. The Stenographer doesn't know
the Intern's name. The Stenographer thinks she would like

to name a baby something ancient and rich.
Her stomach grumbles. She is still getting accustomed

to the new ways. She stares at the Intern. Marvels
at the good skin of youth. The Intern brandishes

a spoon, touches the Stenographer's head
like a priest wielding a blessing.

Blueberry, blueberry, blueberry.

Letter by Letter

In his office in the attic, in his favorite khaki pants,
the Archivist carefully sets down the glass case
of his body so as not to rattle the exhibit of his mind.
He wears gloves to stroke the name on the envelope,
the name written in a florid hand trained by long-ago
love. *To live among the dead*, the Archivist thinks.
His eyebrows do a little jig. With fingers strange
to his wife, the Archivist traces the name of the street
in the village that burned. The street wears the name of the flower
the Archivist's mother tucked behind her ear in a photograph
languishing in a desk drawer. The Archivist carries his mind
into each house. Here, the Cook makes love, his hand
brushing flour against his boyfriend's nipple. There,
the Tailor's satisfied song of scissors bisecting
a ream of red. A girl whose mouth makes an O
around which chocolate makes another mouth runs
through the road. The road which runs through
the Archivist's blood. The girl is the Archivist's grandmother
in that she is a story the Archivist tells
himself about how he got here. Under an oak tree,
two dogs fucking. The girl's ice cream is melting.
The Archivist's mind is sticky with history.
Of course, the village burns again. History is
the only road that survives. Downstairs, the Archivist's daughter
is hungry. He restores the dead to their folders. *To live!*
The girls' wails rise through the house like smoke.

Lecture on the History of the House

Before the alphabet, there was the house.

A proto-Semitic hieroglyphic symbol
depicting a house becomes the letter *b*.
beyt, beit. beit lechem. no house : no bread,
no book, no baby, no babble.

b b b b b b b b b b

When the temple was written, the destruction
of the temple was written.

       The house scripts its defense.
       (The house writes the fence.)

In the beginning, there was _____

          A) night   A) tent
          B) day   B) house

A: The letter, scoring the darkness.
Q: In the beginning, what was?

A: The beginning.
Q: What answered the question silence asked?

A: AAAAAAAAAAAAAAAAAAAAAAAAABBBBBBBBB
Q: ▰▰▰▰▰▰▰▰▰▰▰▰▰

the alphabet : ruin of silence

       The only way back: through language, language
       destroying the silence. The shadow language casts

is silence. No language, no shadow. No know, no
no no no no no no.

To ruin your knowing in your mouth
and dress the ruins with your best tongue.

b b b b b b b b b b

First the temple, then the book
leading back to the temple.

So the interior is measured, apportioned.

walled square footage : living space

It is settled then.

> A house is a home
> and other embroidered facts.

It becomes you, your craft.

> Birdhouses, henhouses, doghouses.
> *Like us, like us*, we chirp.

"Who's the bird now?"

The problem with liking is
> the conflation of desire with similarity.

We form our mouths to fence we in.
We fence our forms to mouth we in.

babble : b b b b b b b b b b

Inside the house, the family.
Inside the family, the house.
Inside the tower, the princess
        does not dream
        of the tower.

Theory is a scream slowed by vintage technology.

                            "Touch me," Amira says. "Touch me."

        The model of the house is the size of a house.

    You confuse the conditions
    that make something possible
    with the conditions that make
    something necessary.

You don't see thinking as an emergency.

You own to prove you cannot be owned.
In owning, you sign a contract of possession.

        The ghost tells the story of the house,
        but none of the other tenants know how to listen.

You lock yourself out: morning.
You lock yourself in: night.

Ownership is a chronic condition.

Install a camera to conjugate the strangeness.

        The house draws your speech like a bath: sink,
                yard, repair, astroturf, neighbor, clean, handyman.
                That good good light.

The first bedroom makes you sad.
The second bedroom makes a baby.
In the corner of the living room, the whole globe
spun by children.

It's more than the Accountant told you it would be.

Which came first, the fence or the yard?

Ink on a black page.

A poem wrestles the ghost with its narrow tongue.
    A poem touches the hip of a ghost.
    In the dark, a thousand names bloom.
No country comes of that night.

What is wild? That which cannot be measured.

                                                    Amira! Amira!

Or: to produce a thought of the outside
from the inside and use it as a tunnel.
But you didn't know you were inside.

        Someone laid the new bricks
        around you while you slept.

You skinned animals and adorned your captivity.

Modern architects called the surfaces of their buildings *skins*.

            Your skin was light.
            Your skin was feathers.
            You dreamed of another.

You lit a match.

"Your child named it sun."

House _____

    A) trained
    B) broken

Inside the house, a man hits you.
Then you understand:
your body is the window.
Inside, you are already outside.

Next door, the Soloist domesticates a tune.

Poetry is a door without a house.

    Theory is productive of the known.
    Poetry is productive of the unknown.

        How, then, do you know
        what is true? These walls, this foundation,
        in the pages of glossy magazines.
        The newspapers scratch their heads.
     Again, the hunters, budgeting.

At the end of the day, you return to what is not common.

What is desire fulfilled?

    A) satisfaction
    B) rot

The man reaches through his woman.
        The sound of a thousand plates shattering.

        A butterfly impaled by a human name
        tumbles through the light like an angel.

                Amira sits under a tree, unpinning the names from things.

The house is without simile.
Inside, everything is alike.

                She releases the names to the wind.
                The wind churns the names to pigment,
                carries the colors off like

b b b b b b b b b b

Oh, I know what a house is.
A house is my knowing.

Knowing is faith absent doubt.

        When doubt is cleaved from faith,
        where does it go?

A caucus of ghosts, cackling—

        Debtor, debtor
        Put on your best sweater
        The magic's fled, the milk's gone bad
        There's nothing left but weather.

Because you needed a fence to limit your loneliness.
Because haunting needed a form.

Your dreams become modest, smooth their skirts, stand up.

Your yard, polluted with growth.

The head in your oven,
your most faithful tenant.

Let me turn my face toward my life.
Let me live inside it forever.

A racket of ghosts in a settling structure.

The Dictator's name
in your lover's hand
on the I-beams of your house.

That is the law.

At Night, the Censor Watches His Wife Tuck Their Son into Bed

She pulls the covers

(When the Censor
recalls his childhood,
he recalls the Cook who
worked for his parents
who loved the boy
who was a boy before
he became the Censor.
When the boy's father
and the boy's mother
crowded the living
room with rising voices,
the boy took shelter
in the kitchen where
the Cook powdered
the counter with flour
and rolled the dough
into a long sheet and
took in his hands
the boy's small hands,
teaching him to cover
the top of the pie
with crust, just so.
The boy grew up
and learned the Cook
had been the Cop,
undercover. The Censor
wondered if love was part
of the Cop's assignment.)

up to the boy's chin.

Parable

The woman sits at her kitchen table across from a head of cabbage. The woman's mouth moves quickly, then slowly. She is trying to explain. She cocks her head to the side, listening. She is trying to understand. Now, she is understanding, nods. Each morning they sit like this, the woman and her cabbage. This is how she grows old, her face a lake the wind whispers to, every day its confidence worrying the surface a bit more. On the stove, the percolator sings. The woman worries over the cabbage. She pours two cups of coffee. One sits there, a tranquil lake. At the end of the day, the woman washes the cups, tenderly, as if washing a body. She knows she is washing a body. One evening, the woman's son comes back. It's not important from where. It's not important how long he's been gone. It matters only that time has deposited in him sarin, legislation, microplastics and when he returns, he is no longer a boy who sings softly to the moon. The man follows orders. He wields what he's amassed. On the windowsill, petunias wilt in dissent. Now there is a head on the floor, smashed as if cabbage. Now there is a witnessing head, silent as cabbage.

(The boy is the state. The cup is you. No, the boy is your lover. The cabbage farmer is you. Or the woman is a lesson. The cabbage is you. No. Oh, the many ways to misread. Or that other risk, the greater one, and what you'd have to do with it—)

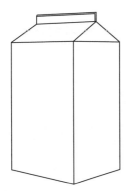

Do you believe in the nation?

Have you ever loved an alien?

Who represents you? In what state?

Was the war civil?

Was the Guard handsome?

When was your greatest depression?

What would John Steinbeck say?

When was the golden era?

Where do you think you are going with that laminated prayer?

Where does the dream of freedom take place?

Hotline

Feeling lonely, you call the hotline.
A voice consoles you, promises a lover
in five to seven business days. In five
to seven business days, the Accountant
arrives at your door. You want your lover. *I want
my lover!* you scream, pounding your fists.
The Accountant smiles. You lust after dental
insurance. You wax your bikini line, bleach
your grammar, shine your dark, make it sing. Your private
property gleams. The Accountant is pleased.
In bed, he counts your teeth like stars.
My country, you learn to say, when you want
your lover. *My country*, the Accountant replies. You are proud
of this marriage you've made. You open your mouth
to show the Accountant your grief. Inside each grief,
a well of ink. The Accountant collects
forty-seven drops. *For good measure*,
he explains. Now that he's paid
his highest compliment, you are ready
to ask for what you've always wanted.
Tell me about the war, you say, laying your head
on his chest. He rations you
dusty Englishes: *margarine, tangerine,
tourniquet*. You forget your hunger
holding them in your mouth. You redecorate
your living room. Red velvet
curtains and a fainting couch you found
discarded on a street corner. To make use
of the couch, you restrict your oxygen.
The Accountant beams. *My country.*
My country. You pour the good river
into your front yard. *Home*, you purr,
petting your property taxes. Late one night,

the hotline calls. There's been a mistake.
They will send your lover right over. *Oh, no,*
you say gazing at your Accountant,
sleep training his breath. *Don't worry*
about it. Things are fine as they are. You hang
up the phone, turn off the light.
Your alarm clock sounds its sparrow call
and a sparrow crashes into your window.

Object Lesson

You learn to recognize beauty by its frame.
In the gilded hall, in the gilded frame, her milky neck

extended as she peers over the drawn bath. A target,
a study, a class: to be beautiful,

she requires you. You should save her, no matter the price.
No matter the price, the Curator will take it. Acquisition makes him

good. He hangs the woman's image
in the museum, where schoolchildren stand

before it, anointed with lessons in color and feeling. *Pay
attention*, the Teacher scolds the fidgeter in back. *Bad,*

the child whose movement dilates her own beauty, the child
whose wails call to his mother, most beautiful of all. *Eyes this way,*

the teacher syrups. All that grows, rots. Good little stillnesses,
guardians-to-be. If you are good, one day

an embossed invitation will arrive at the door of the house
you own. You will sit next to the Curator, light

chattering along the chandeliers, your napkin shaped like a swan.
To protect your silk, you snap its neck with flourish. The blood, beautiful,

reddening your cheeks as you slip into the chair drawn just for you. *Sit*, the chair says
to the patron. *Stand*, to the Guard. The Guard shifts on blistered feet. *She loves you,*

she loves you not. The children pluck the daisy bald,
discard their little sun in the gutter.

Minuet

It is snowing. It was snowing. It is
snowing, still. The snow stills
the day's little dramas. The snow
covers lightly, is light. The days are little,
largely night. Where were dramas
of light, now only snow. Out there,
a room we are all inside. Stilled,
the now presses, blanketing us
like snow. The room is a past.
It contains only a blanket. The now
is a song, passing like light.
The room was a world. You were once
contained, singing. When the room
warms will you still sing the snow?
The world's was once is, will be
our light. And you, passing through,
lightly, like snow. It was not warm.
It is days past night.

The Dictator signs the form and a woman
is disappeared into the past.

Sense and Sensibility

To feel alive, the Intern wears fishnet tights.
No one ever asks her to do anything.
Then everyone asks her to do all things at once.
In lieu of pay, she is exposed. *Lucky*
is the word the Human Resource used when he called
to confirm that she would, indeed, become the Intern,
his voice swelling like a green balloon.
When a dapper colleague tramples her glasses,
the Intern does not become beautiful. In the Intern's life,
debt is the protagonist. Her mother sells skincare
to her church group. Her church group sells skincare
to her mother. Skincare clogs her pores, the basement
of her family home, the hallways, the conversations
that struggle to squirm free like children
stumbling in a deflating bouncy castle. Nothing
is fun. One morning, a man with a mustache and a badge
delivers the eviction notice. Suddenly, the skincare is homeless.
The Intern watches puppy videos and ignores requests for money.
She screens her mother's calls. This morning, no one asks
the Intern to do anything. The Intern finds a penny
on the floor of the break room, tucks it under her tongue.
It tastes like purpose. The Board Chair enters, asks for her name.
Her language closes around the smooth metal.

Lecture on Confessional Poetry

Father, she wrote, and so became beautiful.

To confess
           is to offer the territory of your elsewhere
      to the Dictator's compass.

Wave the red flag of your interior.
The army stations around its perimeter.

Cops populate their websites with headshots.

               Call it *good*.

                                          Amira is not good.
                                                      Is.

      If you know something, call.
      If you see something, say.

The grid of reason makes you mad.
Your saying makes you seen.

You come to your senses like you come home to a two-car garage.

You live in the attic but don't burn down the house.

               "Was your candle the dream of a greater kindling?
                                       Was your poem?"

On TV, the war is on.
The war is off
somewhere far away.

Your feelings squat in the distance
between you and the war.

The distance between you and the war is your country.
The war is your country.

You think of this as nuance.

That you think about the war makes you human.

To be human is to endow lines with meaning
and make others susceptible.

Scrap of flag, square of quilt.

You tease your thought into a nest.
You move into your head.
It's a perfectly good attic.
You've never felt more at home.

You seal your letters, send them off.

This is your war effort.
This is your poem.

"I read between your lines."

Centuries of study
    have not yielded
        a poem's definition.

Thank G-d.

Which came first, the nation or the flag?

Oh, Father.

All over the country, volunteers gather
to stuff good words with newsprint.

      The Intern helps for an hour, then takes off,
      her pockets bulging with pilfered language.

           (If you need to find the Intern,
           follow the trail of stuffed words.)

To confess is to set yourself out to be destroyed.

Attached as you are to your own innocence,
you will die to preserve it.

                                          Speech acts.

A bad deed built a state.

A congregation assembles at the edges.

      Red composing your cheeks.

      A herd of mouths
      waterlogged by wanting
           what they will not name.

Unhusbanded,
           you could be anybody's bride.

Men change your name
with their limited mouths.

From now on, answer to that.

      At the DMV
      At the church
      At the airport
      At the Accountant's office
      At the pharmacy

The Guard's looping cursive, pristine.
You know the script.

When asked what you've done,
you find it hard to account for yourself.

You account for yourself.

      You were there.
      Then you were less.

           "If you can't perceive me, does that mean I'm not here?"

Which came first, her whiteness or the soldiers?

      If she forgives her father in language,
                forgive her father.

      If, in language, she does not forgive her father,
                forgive her.

To name yourself is not to declare your innocence.

To name yourself is to commit yourself
      to the task of your exoneration.

           The name is the guilt.

Death cleanses the name.

        Your funeral is exquisite.
        Linen tablecloths, lilies.
        You thought of everything.

    Attention.

The light instruments:

    Camera.
    Gun.
    Cliché.

Cliché: the sound the camera makes in shooting you.

Amira, doused in darkness.

You send your image to your lover,
who presses his body close to another.

The body requires a name for admission.
A border disrupts a name.
A name change is a border-crossing.
The name increases.
The body is cast aside.

"Look how you've recast the body in language,
so as not to lose what you've destroyed.
Look how you've made language a monument
to your destruction and called it memory.*"*

    Taken as you were
   into so many mouths,
you became the anthem.

Language is the perimeter
of the interior. Confessing, you
fence yourself in, you you you,
yard the woods of your elsewhere.

Inside, pronounless. Then, yolked to I-you.

Now that you are you, you are
the I's guardian.
              I is you, is not.

      A thief thinned with death wish.

You, elsewhere,
              waving
the white flag. We wear your hair
      in a locket, covet
your fingernails in an ivory box.

The heirloom of you makes us we.
If not: hunted.

                        Only the living can be so stingy with form.

      There is imagination. The seed
      dreamt it up. Rattled your glass
      core and worldward shard:
      the word, instrument to sift the dead
      through the narrow frame of your intelligence.

To pluck a word and give it to you.
                    Without which, not you.

                          Without which, magic.

You know where you buried you,
then you lose track,
go looking—

conscripted by her breath's thin draft,
conscripted by its absence.

Blue

came late to
language once
we were

thrashing the sea
was wine-
dark flash

of wing
and nothing
was the same

the sea
kissed the
sky and now

day is then
night is
more what did

you lose
in becoming
family what

dazzling otherwise
do I name
when I

address you

[AMIRA FACES THE WALL. SHE WILL NOT TURN, CANNOT.]

Do you believe in G-d?

Yes.

What is G-d?

G-d is what I walk toward when I walk out into my unknowing.

L'Origine du monde

Quiet as it's kept, everyone
but the Censor knows the Stenographer
is fucking the Censor's wife.
The Stenographer seizes the Censor's
wife's face suspended above her like a moon
and pulls it close. Three words
conduct a private heat between them.
The women climb the bluest hour with their moans,
then shudder into silence in the Censor's bed.
From above, you might mistake them for bodies
strewn across a field in a reenactment of the war
the Dictator worships—where men come weekly,
giddy with guns and myth. They make
of their imaginations a tomb
and lie there. Having left behind the wives
who sewed their revolutionary collars, the men die,
then drink a beer. The Censor has left the city
for a weekend retreat where he will learn
to parse permissible evil from the other kind.
The women, too, conspire toward pleasure.
They find it in his absence.

I Love My Body More Than Other Bodies

is a line from a poem that darts up the Curator's belly
and nests in that organ between what one knows
and what one does like how a name lodges between
body and soul—or so the Curator's grandmother said,
which always made the Curator think
of that impossibly thin breast pocket
on men's dress shirts. One morning, the Curator
was holding his nephew while his sister fussed
with the contraption of her outfit, and the boy slid a paper heart
into that pocket of the Curator's shirt. All day,
through meetings and cocktails, his chest itched
as though the twisted muscle were trying
to reject the foreign form. (Maybe that is language:
the shape that unsettles the thing itself. Lucky—but no
less irritant—if applied with love.) Tonight is the grand opening,
and the Curator's whole body itches like a mind
careening from sleep. *A national pride*, the Dictator
called the museum, inviting the other dictators to revel.
It goes without saying that the Curator despises the Dictator,
appreciates the funding. The museum is shaped like a house.
It wasn't the Curator's idea, but the architecture did inspire
an installation of a century's worth of living rooms
in the lobby. In the lobby, the Curator can't stand the small talk.
He stuffs his mouth with canapés and nods at the Board Chair
whose lips make remarkable shapes. He thinks of Miró.
He endures an hour, then lubricates another with champagne.
The museum is not a house. Having put in his time, the Curator
slips out, lifting his beloved shoe to step over a man sleeping
on the street. The Curator sleeps well. He worked so hard
to bring this about. He works so hard.

Graveyard Shift

When the Soldier went to war, he wanted
to go home. He wrote a letter to his Mother,
which the Mailman carried over the mountain
into the Censor's office. *Dear Mother,*
his mother read.

I hope you are

        missing

I know

  I am

        something beautiful
    ruined

       Your Son

Of course she understood. The Doctors
concocted nostalgia, the Poets dreamt up modernity.
The Mothers went on understanding.

When the Soldier occupied his mother,
she sang a folksong to her belly. He kicked.
She called it *dancing.* Late one night, something
was born.

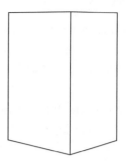

[AMIRA PULLS HER CHAIR CLOSER TO THE TABLE,
CLEARS HER THROAT AS THOUGH SHE IS THE ONE CONVENING THIS MEETING.]

What if we burn your books?

I will write more books.

What if we burn the forests?

The books I've written have already changed me.

And if we burn you?

My ash will be ink on the page of the earth.

Lecture on Loneliness

The first woman was not burdened with firsts, only was.
Not yet bound by a name, uncalled for.
Only history makes her lonely, only after makes her first.

>   Of course this is an origin story—
>   lonely as any birth.

Loneliness: the distance
between history and what history might have been.

The thread unspools.
The umbilical, severed.

"Why do your books
clog the doorway to the past?"

A blanket of yellow petals.

The rain: little fists
beating back the dead
who want only to braid your hair.

You built a world against such softness.

You arranged an alphabet against loneliness.

"I scale your walls. That is my practice."

In the schools, children line up, chant:

>   To be   alone, among
>   To be   without, among
>   To be   among, without
>   To be   without, alone

To trade your wonder for knowing, gladly.

To confuse the loss of nothing with the loss of nothing.

You knew. Then you knew more.
You diminished the world with your knowing.

The distance between you and your quiet grows.

A ladder, receding into the sky.

The first woman of your life
stitches her face into your sleep
like your grandmother
stitched coins into the lining of her coat, and ran.

You wake. Run through the woods, jingling.

The sound of your skirt accompanies you.

You forget your sisters.

You make of the hour a horse, ride off.

"I've ridden those horses, your lost hours."

The children lick honey from the letters.

The righteous man climbs the tree.
On the first branch, he cuts off his hair.
At the top, he discards his body.

A person can be with a word like they can be with a body:

> Wash it.
> Accompany it.
> Be changed by its nearness.

The woman lays all the lavender at your feet.
The browned fields balk.

You scatter flowers along the sidewalks,
paint a mural of a rain forest in a prison.

The years ascend the mirror
like sea level.
A face breaks off like an iceberg.
It is your mother's.

The years add.
The years subtract.

You are always wrong.

"Take me with you!"

You populate your memory with her scent and her language.
You remember so little.

You are in bed.
In a room down the hall:
words exchanged in the dark.
Distance sands the words to noise.

The room is the world.

Three daffodils later, and you've shed your memory like a skin.

No matter how much you water it, the stone refuses its flowering.

> You strike the stone.
> It withholds the river.

The letters are lanterns
and lead to no house.

The townspeople emptied their language
and could no longer meet each other there.

"Was the language empty?
Or was it open?"

The truth lost its coordinates.

A weathered man, dusting snow from the ridge of his year.

The name of an old lover assails him.
No! The light hurts.

He closes her name like a book.

"If you excise me from your memory,
I will enter your blood."

Little capillaries, little trees.

Little heart governed by a solitary rain cloud.

The only laws:

    Be radiant.
    Be heavy.
    Be green.

Tonight, the dead light up your mind
like an image of your mind on a scientist's screen.

                              "The scientists don't know—and too much."

In the town square, in the heart of night (a delicacy
like the heart of an artichoke), a man dances
cheek to cheek with the infinite blue.

Of course, his mother's death blooms
so much larger in his life
than her life ever did. An endless flowering,
what is gone. Scant still against what will
never be. No language
for the engulfing mouths of the not-become.

After you, no one asks.

Look how you shredded the quiet with your promises.

    Look how you lost her, anyway.

        Look, now—no quiet to accompany you.

Your words are sisterless.

No, no one asks after you.

A finger plumbing the depths of your night.

It rained in your room.
You mistook the ceiling for sky.

The rain allots you just one glass.
It has to last your life.

The rain extinguishes summer.

You behead the flowers.
You forget their names.

      To share what you love with one you admire,
      and be scorned: fingernails along your
      innermost parts.

Every embrace, a rehearsal of separation.

Your mother's life, halved like a peach,
the stubborn pit exposed to weather.

One morning, in a shop, you meet someone who wears your hair,
who speaks your name like the one who named you.

The bells on the door clink as you leave with your butter.

To be suspended between oneself
like the man who balanced on a wire between mountains
then tumbled toward death like a helicopter seed.

"A burial is
a seed planted in the wrong season."

To be the wrong season.

To work all your life in the name of family.
    Each labored hour a brick
    in the road leading you away.

"A name is not a leash.
I will be in the field
watching the tulips grow."

The women come with aprons full of hours.

The world aches, unpassed over by the eyes of the dead.

The dead have no eyes.

Lonely, lonely living.

"Do all of your antics recover the radiance, and was it worth it?"

Go on, hang the stars from the sky.
This world is a pageant of your making.

The hour of forgetting is a brown hour.
The house of forgetting looks like any other.

The trees are dark and full of language.
The trees speak, but not to you.

First, the year without music.

Then, in a minor key, in a dead language, the woman sang this song:

We were the last people on earth.
We made a world between us.
We spent the earth.
I made my body a cloak and took you in.
In all that you, I lost myself.
I traveled the length of my interior, and there I wasn't.
My language was a symptom of a history I couldn't touch.
I petitioned the dead for company.
No one came.
The butterflies fell like autumn leaves.
The shells washed up on the beach, empty as G-d's ears.
We were the last.
I called this life.

"Here, a door.
And like that, we went."

The Edmond Jabès epigraph is Rosmarie Waldrop's translation from *The Book of Questions*.

The end of "[The original gesture]"—"She's in your hands now"—bears in mind Toni Morrison's Nobel lecture.

"Lecture on Time" is indebted to the thinking of Masha Gessen, Fred Moten, Anthony Reed, Michel-Rolph Trouillot, and Jackie Wang.

"Diet" is with apologies to Robert Hass.

"At Night, the Censor Watches His Wife Tuck Their Son into Bed" is after Robin Coste Lewis and retells an anecdote from Masha Gessen's *The Future Is History*.

The question posed by Amira in *Interrogation Room* [AMIRA PRESSES HER FEET DEEP INTO HER SHOES. HER SHOES ARE TOO SMALL.] moves after Robin D. G. Kelley's *Freedom Dreams: The Black Radical Imagination*.

"Lecture on Confessional Poetry" holds in mind advice E. J. Koh received from a poetry professor, as Koh relays in *The Magical Language of Others*: "You don't have to forgive your mother. I'm not telling you to forgive her. But the poem must forgive her, or the poem must forgive you for not." The poem is also informed by the work of Kamran Javadizadeh on confessional poetry, as well as the scholarship of Krista Thompson and Simone Browne on anti-Black technologies of light.

"I Love My Body More Than Other Bodies" takes its title from a line in Kaveh Akbar's poem "What Use Is Knowing Anything If No One Is Around."

"Lecture on Loneliness" is indebted to the poetry of Paul Celan, especially Pierre Joris's translation of "Stretto."

Edmond Jabès, *Le Livre des questions*
Huey Copeland, *Bound to Appear*
Kevin Quashie, *The Sovereignty of Quiet*
George Jackson, *Soledad Brother*
The understory's variegated darknesses
Mahmoud Darwish, *Memory for Forgetfulness* (trans. Ibrahim Muhawi)
Solmaz Sharif, *Look*
Black Audio Film Collective, *Handsworth Songs*
Aracelis Girmay, *the black maria*
Paul Celan, *Memory Rose into Threshold Speech* (trans. Pierre Joris)
Mona Hatoum, *Roadworks*
Dionne Brand, *Ossuaries*
סליחות
Canisia Lubrin, *The Dyzgraph*st*
Mariame Kaba, *We Do This 'Til We Free Us*
Natalie Diaz, *Postcolonial Love Poem*
Aimé Césaire, *Cahier d'un retour au pays natal*
A letter sent between hemispheres, a name assembling across the seasons
Édouard Glissant, *Poétique de la relation*
The dispossession of orgasm
Yiyun Li, *Where Reasons End*
The first notes of a song depositing you into another decade
A child falling—that glance up, scouring the beloved face for meaning
The scent of honeysuckle
Christina Sharpe, *In the Wake*
Who read the draft
Who took notes to share
Hortense Spillers, "Mama's Baby, Papa's Maybe: An American Grammar Book"
June Jordan, *His Own Where*
The loitering hands washing a lover's hair
Saidiya Hartman, *Wayward Lives, Beautiful Experiments*
Zaina Alsous, *A Theory of Birds*
Fernando Pessoa, *The Book of Disquiet* (trans. Richard Zenith)

Solomon Ibn Gabirol, שער אשר נסגר

Birds

Gwendolyn Brooks, *Maud Martha*

Where rehearsal yields to improvisation

How my mother mothered the aloe and so it became my sibling

Kader Attia, *Rochers Carrés*

What grief knows about love

Latifa Echakhch, *À chaque stencil une revolution*

The typography of picket signs

The company of dreamers

Osip Mandelstam, *Voronezh Notebooks* (trans. Andrew Davis)

The girl darting out from the crowd to turn the teargas canister around

M. NourbeSe Philip, *She Tries Her Tongue, Her Silence Softly Breaks*

Theresa Hak Kyung Cha, *Dictee*

The way the body languaged *thank you* before the tongue had the words

The flapping mouth of the screen door when you leave

Michel-Rolph Trouillot, *Silencing the Past*

Acknowledgments—

Thank you to the editors of the following journals, where poems from *Civil Service* first appeared, sometimes in earlier versions:

> *Granta*—"Letter by Letter" and "Lecture on Loneliness"
> *The Nation*—"Apples"
> *Poetry*—"Object Lesson," "Preferential Treatment," and "Lecture on the History the House"
> *Virginia Quarterly Review*—"Death Revises Badly" and "Meaning Well"
> *Washington Square Review*—"Hotline"

✳

> Surely you see that these lines are the way they are
> because I do not know how to thank you.
> —PAUL CELAN (TRANS. PIERRE JORIS)

Hannah Aizenman, Kaveh Akbar, Elizabeth Alexander, Arielle Angel, Bridget Bergin, Chase Berggrun, Ari Brostoff, Christian Campbell, Nora Caplan-Bricker, Jos Charles, Cortney Lamar Charleston, Natalie Diaz, Cynthia Friedman, Nathan Goldman, Jacqueline Goldsby, Miriam Halachmi (ז״ל), Pierre Joris, Annette Joseph-Gabriel, Ilya Kaminsky, Robin D. G. Kelley, Key Jo Lee, Canisia Lubrin, Oana Marian, Kobena Mercer, Lauren Meyer, Dunya Mikhail, Lisa Monroe, Saretta Morgan, Valzhyna Mort, Bridget Ngcobo, Maryam Parhizkar, Tina Post, Anthony Reed, Stéphane Robolin, Doris Salcedo, Evie Shockley, Jodie Stewart-Moore, R. A. Villanueva, Andy, Elijah, Ezra, Genia, Guy, Izzy, Jessica, Laura, Lucien, Melody, Noah, Noémie, Salomé, Shayla, Sofie, Sophie, you whom I miss; all at Graywolf, Jeff Shotts, Chantz Erolin, especially, beyond; *plus près*: my parents, myemilychu, Zuzu, Ben.

Reader—You revised this text. Thank you.

[AMIRA FACES YOU.]

Did you think it was good?

The torturer wore pearls.

Then why did you write it?

I knew, one day, we wouldn't be together.

Claire Schwartz is the culture editor of *Jewish Currents*. She is the winner of a Whiting Award and her writing has appeared in *Granta*, the *Nation*, *Poetry*, *Virginia Quarterly Review*, and elsewhere.

The text of *Civil Service* is set in Garamond Premier Pro.
Book design by Rachel Holscher.
Composition by Bookmobile Design and Digital
Publisher Services, Minneapolis, Minnesota.
Manufactured by McNaughton & Gunn on FSC-certified acid-free paper.